SCIENCE FACTORY

SOUND
& MUSIC

JON RICHARDS

STARGAZER BOOKS

New edition published in 2005

Designed and produced by
Aladdin Books Ltd

First paperback edition published in
the United States in 2005 by
Stargazer Books
c/o The Creative Company
123 South Broad Street
P.O. Box 227
Mankato, Minnesota 56002

Design
David West
Children's Book Design

Designer
Flick Killerby

Illustrators
Ian Moores & Ian Thompson

Printed in U.A.E.

Cataloging-in-Publication data is
available from the Library of
Congress.

ISBN: 1-932799-72-9

ABOUT THE BOOK

Sound and Music examines the basic aspects of sound, as well as its more complex and practical uses. By following the projects carefully, the readers are able to develop their practical skills, while at the same time expanding their scientific knowledge. Other ideas then offer them the chance to explore each aspect further to build up a more comprehensive understanding of the subject.